AUSTIN & LEIGH PUBLISHING
Philadelphia, PA
austinleigh.com | info@austinleigh.com

Copyright © 2014


ISBN: 978-0692343913

# Laz the Magic Boy and Santa

by Debbie Boutwell

Once upon a time there was a very special little boy named Laz. Now Laz looked like any other boy; he had red hair, a dimple in his cheek when he smiled, and he was always full of fun. But there was one thing about Laz that was different from most other boys; he had a bag of magic things that he always kept with him. His bag was filled with things that many people thought were just ordinary, but the truth is that even though they looked

like ordinary everyday things they had magical powers. And the really interesting thing about Laz's bag was that every time he opened it something different would come out of it.

Laz spent many weekends at his grandparents' homes and almost every time he came to see them he would have an adventure. He had a Grandmom Donna, a Granddad Bill, a Grammy Debbie and a Papaw Ken. Laz had a Mama and a Papa, and an Uncle Brent, Aunt Megan, an Aunt Ky, an Aunt

Brooke and Uncle Jeff. All of these people loved Laz very much and they often shared adventures with him.

One day while Laz was visiting with his Papaw and his Grammy over Christmas break, he was helping his Grammy make Christmas cookies. Laz was standing on the step stool that let him reach the counter, decorating some sugar cookies to look like Christmas trees, reindeer, stars, and bells. "I wonder when Santa is coming," Laz asked.

"I imagine it will not be until you are fast asleep," his Grammy said.

Laz didn't say much after that, but when the cookies were finished and cooling on the counter he climbed down and went into the den.  Grammy followed him and watched as he pulled his bag of magic things down off the table and sat down on the floor in front of the Christmas tree.  He began to look in the bag as if to take stock of the contents.

"What's up, Laz?" Grammy asked.

"I think I just need to be ready in case Santa comes early tonight," he replied.

"Early?" Grammy asked.

"Yes, he just might need for me to help him." Laz said very seriously.

"Well," Grammy said, seriously, "it's always important to be ready." Grammy turned her head so Laz wouldn't see her smile.

Later that evening after the whole family had gathered for dinner, Granddad Bill patted his tummy and said "Boy, am I full!" Then Papaw Ken yawned and said, "I am so sleepy."

Laz's Mom looked at Laz and said

"I think it is time for one little boy to go to bed." So Laz kissed everyone good night, gathered up his stuffed duck, Filbert, his bag of magic things and said, "I guess maybe Santa won't come early tonight."

Laz went off to bed and Grammy followed behind. "Santa is so busy tonight. I wouldn't worry too much about him not coming early."

"I know he is busy, that is why I thought he would come early," Laz explained patiently to her. Grammy kissed him goodnight and went back into the den with the other grownups.

Laz lay very still and listened to the

grownups talking, but just as he was about to drift off to sleep he heard the tiniest tinkle he had ever heard. He began to listen more carefully and soon he heard the sound of something in front of the house. Laz peeked out the window to see if he could tell what it was and his breath caught in his throat as he saw the feet of some large animal jump up onto the roof of the porch.

Most boys would have been afraid, but not Laz; he was very brave when unusual things happened. So he got out of bed, slipped on his rocket ship slippers and picked up his bag of magic

things. He peeked out into the hall and saw that there was a soft glow in the den but almost no noise. "Well," he said to himself, "I guess everyone has gone to bed." Laz walked down the hall until he came to the den and peeked into the room.

There, he saw a little man dressed in red, with a long white beard standing in front of the Christmas tree. The man looked right at Laz, put his finger to his lips and whispered, "Are you ready?"

Laz nodded, and walked right up to Santa and put his hand in Santa's. "I knew you were coming," Laz said.

"OK," Santa said in a no-nonsense

voice. "We need to get started if we are going to finish before morning."

Laz grabbed some of the cookies off the Santa plate, dropped them in his bag, grabbed his coat and said, "Let's go!"

Laz and Santa stepped right up to the fireplace, and Santa said, "Hold your breath and close your eyes." Laz did just as he was told and when he opened his eyes he was not standing in the cozy warm den where his Grammy, Pa-paw and Ky lived. He was on the roof. He blinked his eyes to clear them and looked in wonder at the biggest sleigh

he had ever seen.  He also looked at an enormous reindeer with huge antlers.

"But I thought you had lots of reindeer?" he asked Santa.

"I do but someone left the barn open last night and they all got out except Rudolph," Santa explained.  "My elves and I have looked all day and we are out of time," Santa said.  "We have too much to do tonight and we will never get all the presents delivered without our Reindeer.  I have sent the elves out to make some deliveries to the older kids and teenagers.  Rudolph and I have done all we could, but when I

remembered that you had your bag of
magic things I knew just where we
should go for help.  I need for you to
help me round up
the missing rein-
deer and then
we will need
some help
delivering the
rest of the
presents.  Do you
think you can
help me?"  Santa
asked.
"Of course,"  Laz

replied, and he reached into his magic bag and pulled out what looked like an ordinary telescope. He put it to his eye and looked all around the yard. "Not here," he declared and crawled into the sleigh.

Santa got in beside him and called for Rudolph to take off. "AWAY!" he shouted and off Rudolph flew. Laz sat beside him, with his magic telescope to his eye, scouring the countryside.

After what seemed like a long time, Laz pulled the telescope down and pointed to a wooded area below. Santa nodded and using the reins steered the

sleigh down toward the forest.

As they got closer to the ground, Laz was enthralled by the sparkling snow and the dark green of the evergreen trees of the forest. "Why, where else would they be, but in a Christmas tree forest?" Santa said. It was as silent as could be, when the sleigh set down on the soft blanket of snow. "We must be very quiet," Santa whispered to Laz.

Laz nodded and reached into his bag of magic things and pulled out what looked like a simple flashlight. But was in reality a magic flashlight that cast a

special glow that looked just like moonlight over the ground of the forest.

Then, he reached in again and pulled out a rope, which looked like a simple everyday rope. Santa motioned Laz to follow him into the forest and they quietly started into the cold woods. Laz shined his magic flashlight all around and everywhere he aimed it a soft silver silver glow reflected off the trees and snowy ground. Santa and Laz had not gone very far when Laz stopped. He looked at Santa and pointed to an opening in the thicket. There they saw eight

reindeer pawing at the ground. Santa pointed to Laz's rope and Laz made a lasso out of it and swung it over his head. When he threw it, the rope seemed to expand into a lasso large enough to encircle all the reindeer at once. When the lasso settled over the reindeer Laz pulled the magic rope tight (but not too tight) and together, he and Santa walked over to the reindeer.

"Do you know how much trouble you have caused me tonight?" Santa asked. The reindeer seemed to lower their heads in shame. "Well never

mind, even reindeer like to have adventures, but now we have no time to lose," Santa said. The reindeer lifted their heads proudly and walked two by two back to the sleigh. When they got there they lined up in the proper order and waited to be harnessed up to the sleigh. Rudolph, of course, was in his place of honor at the front.

After they were all firmly attached and prancing in excitement, Santa turned to Laz. "We can take you home first if you want, but it would be such a help if you would go with us

tonight," Santa asked.

Laz was so excited and pleased to help that he immediately shouted a loud resounding "YES!"  So Santa, Laz, and all the reindeer took off into the cold night air.  At each house Santa would ask Laz for something special and Laz would reach into Santa's bag and pull out just the right present for the boy or girl who lived in the house.

When the night was finally turning to dawn and they were coming up to Laz's own house, Santa turned to the little boy and saw that he had fallen fast asleep.  Santa slowed the reindeer,

until they stopped on the roof of Grammy and Papaw's house, and lifted Laz as if he weighed nothing at all. Next thing you know, they were down the chimney and Santa was carefully placing Laz in his very own bed. "Thanks Laz, Magic Boy, for all your help," he whispered. Santa carefully and quietly tiptoed out of Laz's bedroom and put a very special gift under the Christmas tree. And then away he went up the chimney.

Laz awoke early the next morning and went to wake his parents, his grandparents, his Aunt Ky,

and his Uncle Brent, and his Aunt Megan.  They all rushed into the den and looked with wonder at the presents under the Christmas tree.  Just then the doorbell rang and in came Grandmom Donna, Granddad Bill, and Aunt Brooke
loaded down with more presents.

"I think it must have snowed last night!" Granddad Bill exclaimed. "Why, there is a sparkly white powder drifting off the roof," he explained.

Laz just smiled and said, "Santa must have brought some with him last night."  After all the presents were

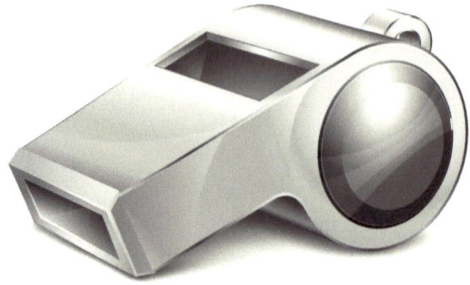

opened and there was just one present left.  Papaw Ken pulled it out from under the tree and handed it to Laz.  Laz carefully opened it up and pulled out a little toy sled, a whistle, and a snow globe.  Everyone came closer and looked at the snow globe. Inside the globe there was a little forest with an opening in the middle, and in the opening, eight tiny reindeer.  Laz pulled out a note from the box and gave it to his Papa to read.

Papa read, "Dear Laz, thanks for all your help last night, the snow globe is to remind you of our adventure.  The toy sled is just in case you need some transportation in the future and the whistle is so that you can always call for help if you need it. Put them in your bag of magic things. Be good and remember, you are Laz the Magic Boy. Love, Santa." When he finished everyone in the family turned and looked at Laz with their eyes and mouths wide open. Laz looked at his family and just smiled and shrugged his shoulders. "I told you Santa would come early." Then he turned and began to play with his brand new toys.